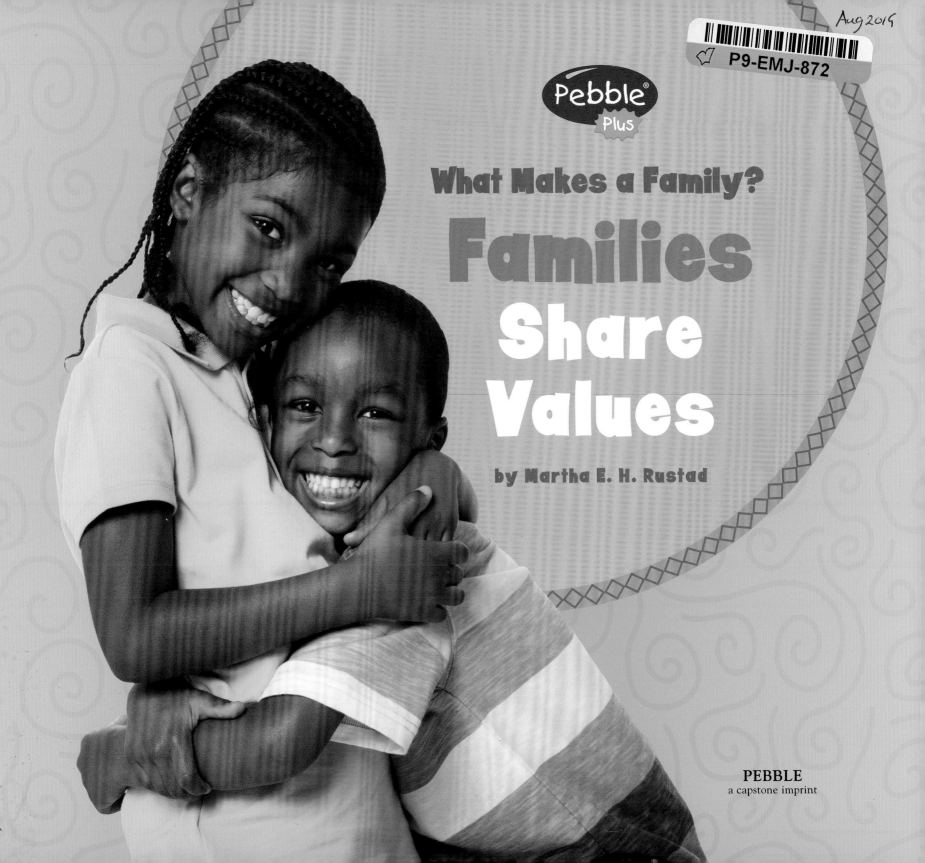

Pebble® Plus

What Makes a Family?

Families Share Values

by Martha E. H. Rustad

PEBBLE
a capstone imprint

Pebble Plus is published by Pebble
1710 Roe Crest Drive,
North Mankato, Minnesota 56003
www.mycapstone.com

Library of Congress Cataloging-in-Publication Data
Library of Congress Cataloging-in-Publication Data is available on the Library of Congress website.
ISBN 978-1-9771-0905-7 (library binding)
ISBN 978-1-9771-1053-4 (paperback)
ISBN 978-1-9771-1275-0 (eBook PDF)

Editorial Credits
Marissa Kirkman, editor; Cynthia Della-Rovere, designer;
Eric Gohl, media researcher; Tori Abraham, production specialist

Image Credits
iStockphoto: FatCamera, 9, fstop123, 15, monkeybusinessimages, 5, Pahis, 21, Steve Debenport, 11; Shutterstock: anek.
soowannaphoom, 7, Hogan Imaging, 1, KatsiarynaKa2, 17, Monkey Business Images, 13, 19, Zurijeta, cover
Design Elements: Shutterstock

All internet sites appearing in back matter were available and accurate when this book was sent to press.

Note to Parents and Teachers
The What Makes a Family? set supports national standards related to social studies. This book describes and illustrates the values shared by different families. The images support early readers in understanding the text. The repetition of words and phrases helps early readers learn new words. This book also introduces early readers to subject-specific vocabulary words, which are defined in the Glossary section. Early readers may need assistance to read some words and to use the Table of Contents, Glossary, Read More, Internet Sites, Critical Thinking Questions, and Index sections of the book.

Printed and bound in China.
001654

Table of Contents

What Are Values?

This is my family. We have values that we believe in and follow. A value is an important idea. Many adults teach values to the children in their family.

Values in the World

Sean learns to be polite
with others. He uses good
manners with everyone.
He chooses to be kind to all
of his teachers and classmates.

Tina learns about faith.

Her family goes to church.

They say prayers and sing

songs. A leader reads stories.

Luna learns to give to others. She and her mom serve a meal to people at a shelter. Her dad and sister help too. They bring clothes for people in need.

Luis learns to try new things. He and his family travel to new places. Luis hikes in the woods for the first time. His dad asks him to try different food.

Jin learns about teamwork.

His dad coaches his soccer team.

Jin and his teammates learn to

work together. Jin passes

the ball. His teammate scores!

Values at Home

Amaya learns about honesty. She and her stepbrother break a lamp. They tell their dad the truth. Dad is proud of them for being honest.